of
# HOLY
*Saturday*

**Immaculate** Heart of Mary
Botwell House
**Botwell** Lane, Hayes
**Middlesex**, UB3 2AB

# Our
# LADY
## of
# HOLY
## Saturday

### Awaiting the Resurrection
### With Mary and the Disciples

## CARDINAL CARLO MARTINI

### Liguori
LIGUORI, MISSOURI

*Imprimi Potest:*
Richard Thibodeau, C.Ss.R.
Provincial, Denver Province
The Redemptorists

Published by Liguori Publications
Liguori, Missouri
www.liguori.org
www.catholicbooksonline.com

**Library of Congress Cataloging-in-Publication Data**

Martini, Carlo Maria, 1927–
    [Madonna del Sabato Santo. English]
    Our Lady of Holy Saturday : awaiting the Resurrection with Mary and the disciples / Carlo Martini ; translated by Andrew Tulluch].—Rev. ed.
      p. cm.
    ISBN 0-7648-0927-X
    1. Holy Saturday. 2. Mary, Blessed Virgin, Saint. 3. Faith. I. Title.

BT468 .M2713 2002
242'.35—dc21                                 2002073068

Original title: La Madonna del Sabato Santo
© 2000 ITL spa, Milano, Italy
English language translation:
Title: Our Lady of Holy Saturday
© 2001 St Pauls, UK

Previously published by ST PAULS Publishing, 187 Battersea Bridge Road, London SW11 3A5

Printed in the United States of America
06 05 04 03      5 4 3 2
Revised edition 2002

# Contents

# Introduction

This Pastoral Letter was originally published [in the diocese of Milan] during the year of the Great Jubilee, which ended on January 6, 2001. It was suggested to me, by more than one person, that I should avoid writing a letter that added any new projects to the numerous ones which were already scheduled for the Jubilee Year, such as the Milanese diocesan pilgrimage to Rome.

What we really need at this moment, it seems to me, is a break in our journey: a pause that will help us to catch up with ourselves, have a look around, and find out where we are— a pause that will sustain us as we recover a vision and draw breath on our journey, a little in the manner of the *Letter of Presentation to the Diocese* of *the Forty-Seventh Synod* (1995) and of the letter *Let Us Depart Once More With God* (1996).

What do we mean when we say "take a break"? I am reminded here of a significant moment during the recent journey of John Paul II to Jerusalem. During this journey we saw a Pope, bent under the weight of his years and labors, pause in silence before the Wailing Wall, in great humility, holding in his hand a piece of paper on which was written a request for forgiveness; he placed the piece of paper slowly into one of the gaps between the stones of the Wall, a gesture familiar to millions of Jews, and in so doing he joined the tradition of prayer and suffering of an entire people. We saw him again, a little before his departure, standing in silence and prayer before the Rock of Calvary. We do not need to have been to

Jerusalem to understand what the Pope was doing, as he paused for a moment on his journey, in silent contemplation; it is something that we have all done: pausing silently in contemplation on our journey, in an effort to understand the meaning of all that we have experienced and suffered, opening ourselves to hear what the Spirit has to say to us at the beginning of the new millennium.

This was the way in which I reflected on the meaning of this "Sabbath of Time," the Great Jubilee. The Jubilee—according to the fundamental text found in Leviticus 25:8–17—is in fact the "Sabbath of Sabbaths," the "sabbatical year of the sabbatical years," the year that comes immediately after the seven weeks of years and for this reason participates in the holiness of the Sabbath, the day on which God rests and with him his creatures. This year is the year in which the absolute supremacy of the

Lord over life and all the events of history is proclaimed, the day on which the order of justice and of peace between all people and creation is restored, according to the plan of the Eternal One. This year is the year in which everything that is not in harmony and that has accumulated over time are brought back into balance; all the fields are allowed to lie fallow, goods are restored to their original owners, debtors are released from their debts, and slaves are freed. In this pause the religious sense of time is expressed; it is a pause which recalls the dominion of God over the entire cosmos and all human doings.

During the Jubilee Year, therefore, we call to mind the precious gift of the "Sabbath" to the people of Israel in whose faith lie the holy roots of the Church (Rom 11:16,18); in the Sabbath we rediscover the holiness of time, wrapped in God's blessing. We are able to cast a trusting eye over all the events of history, because the Sabbath reminds us that the God of the Covenant is faithful and never tires of caring for his people as they journey towards the Promised Land.

For us Christians, however, there is another "Sabbath" which lies at the very heart of our faith: Holy Saturday, set within the Paschal Triduum of the death and resurrection of Jesus and marked out as a time of intense suffering, waiting, and hope.

Holy Saturday is a Sabbath of deep silence. For the first disciples it was a time of mourning; their hearts were still full of the sorrowful images connected with Jesus' death, a death which seems to spell the end of their messianic hopes. It is also the Sabbath of Mary, the faithful Virgin, the Ark of the Covenant, the Mother of Love. For her Holy Saturday was a time of tears but also an experience of the strength of faith, as she worked to sustain the fragile hope of the disciples. It seemed to me that reflecting on Holy Saturday—as experienced by the apostles but above all by Mary—might help us to recover our vision, catch our breath and begin to see ourselves as pilgrims in the Sabbath of Time journeying towards the Sunday without sunset.

It was on this Sabbath—which stands between the sadness of the Cross and the joy of Easter—that the disciples tasted the silence of God, the full weight of his apparent defeat; they were scattered because of the Master's absence, the Master who all thought had become a prisoner of death. It was on this Sabbath that Mary kept watch, guarding within her that total trust she had in God's promises and in the hope she had in the power that raises the dead.

I would like us to enter the grace of the Jubilee Year through the door of Holy Saturday: in the disciples we recognize the confusion, the yearnings, and the fears that characterize our lives as believers as we approach the end of the century and begin the new millennium; in Our Lady of the Sabbath we recognize our own waiting, our own hopes, the faith lived as a continual passage towards the mystery. Mary, the Faithful Virgin, will help us rediscover that it is God's initiative and our faithful openness to his Word which count; Mary, the bride of the Messianic wedding feast, will help us to grasp the value of the communion that unites us as Church—a communion established through the pact which is confirmed by the blood of Jesus—and helps us to strengthen our hope in the Kingdom to come; Mary, Mother of the Crucified, will lead us to a renewed appreciation of the charity through which he handed himself over to death for us, the charity that is the distinguishing mark of a disciple and from which is born the Church of Love.

The disciples and Mary, in their Holy Saturday, can help us understand the passing of the century and millennium so that we can respond with truth, hope, and love to the questions that we all carry within us: where is Christianity headed? Where is the Church that we love headed? In my heart there is an answer to these questions, and I would like to share it with you: we are in the Sabbath of Time; time, that is to say, which has been sanctified by God; holy time, in which we look back at the journey we have so far completed; time in which the future of the promise reveals itself, a future when the "eighth day" of the Lord Jesus' return will come for all. And during this year of grace of the Jubilee we are particularly called to live not outside but within the contradictions that history seems to present to believers.

We will begin our meditation by looking at Holy Saturday from the

perspective of the disciples, bewildered and confused (chapter 1), and
then we will move on to the perspective of Mary, Mother of Jesus (chapter 2), in order to illuminate through
the perspective and inspirational
strength of Mary, the questions the
disciples had and the questions that
we ourselves, with our little faith have,
for our part (chapter 3).

This meditation on Holy Saturday should help believers to answer
the twofold question that is present
in many of us at the beginning of the
millennium: where are we? And:
where are we headed?

This might be an opportunity for
thoughtful nonbelievers—who are
troubled by the same question—to listen to what the faith has to say regarding the meaning of this time and the
meaning of history; the faith does not
offer an ideological plan, but something which is the fruit of a deeply felt
reflection; something which should

come as a breath of fresh and cleaning air; something which stimulates us to carry on seeking and to hope, and to listen to the voice that speaks in silence to whoever searches in honesty.

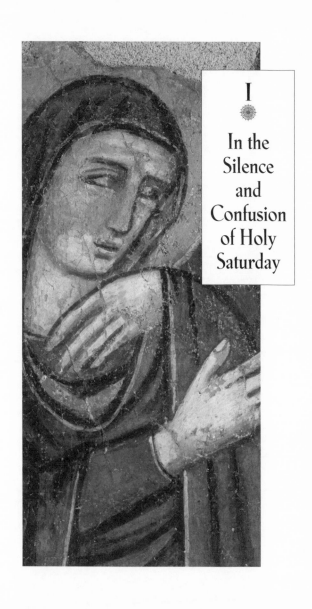

# I

*

In the
Silence
and
Confusion
of Holy
Saturday

L et us first of all try to picture the mood prevailing amongst the disciples the day after Jesus' death; we will then begin to understand our own time in the light of their experience.

## 1. The bewilderment of the disciples

On the Sabbath after the crucifixion of the Master, so it seems to me, the disciples were immersed in utter confusion and dismay. Why were they so bewildered?

Because their Lord and Master had been killed, his call to conversion had not been heard, the authorities had condemned him, and there appeared to be no escape from their predicament; nor could they find anything positive in it. From the Paschal Supper onwards, one unforeseen event had followed another and the disciples had been stunned and silenced. Like the two disciples who walked to Emmaus on the first day of that week, they were sad at heart (Lk 24:17); the forewarnings that they had been given (Jesus had predicted his forthcoming Passion more than once), the deeds that had sustained them up to that point (the Master's miracles, the love that he had shown them at the Last Supper), were now all forgotten. God, it seemed, had become silent, he no longer spoke to them, and his help to understand the unfolding of history was no longer forthcoming. The poor, it seemed, were defeated; justice, it had been proved, did not pay.

To all this, we can add the shame they must have felt because they had disowned the Lord: they saw themselves as traitors, unable to face the present. They no longer had the ability to see things from the perspective of the future; they could see no escape from the catastrophic situation in which all their illusions had come tumbling down; and we must remember that they had not yet encountered the signs that were to shake them from Sunday morning onwards (such as the women finding the empty tomb, see Lk 24:22–23).

## 2. Why should we dwell on Holy Saturday?

We might ask ourselves at this point: why dwell on Holy Saturday? Surely we are now living in the time of the Risen One? Shouldn't we rather draw inspiration from Easter Sunday? Why reflect on the disciples' confusion after the death of Jesus rather than their joy when they encounter the living Lord (see Jn 20:20 "Then the disciples rejoiced when they saw the Lord")?

We are, of course, now living in the time of the Resurrection; the glorious body of the Lord fills the universe with its strength and draws all human creatures to itself so that it can clothe every one in its own incorruptibility. Our fundamental attitude must be one of Easter joy.

And yet, the light of the Risen One, seen by the eyes of faith, is still mingled with the shadow of death. We are already saved in faith and hope (Rom 8:24); our inner selves are already resurrected with Jesus in baptism, but outwardly we remain subject to suffering, illness, and the waning of our powers. The relentless destructive power of sin has been defeated, and yet it continues to affect countless human situations and still causes terrible things to happen. The poor are oppressed, the overbearing triumph, and the meek are despised.

Our situation is similar to that of the two disciples journeying to Emmaus on Easter morning. Jesus is risen, the women have found the empty tomb, the angels have told them not to seek for him among the dead (Lk 24:2–6, 22–23), but their hearts are still heavy: "Oh, how foolish you are, and how slow of heart to believe all that the prophets have declared!" (Lk 24:25). We are like the apostles cowering in the Upper Room, who have already heard talk of the Resurrection and yet remain locked in the room through fear (Jn 20:19).

In other words, the time in which we live is one in which the "Good News" of the Risen Lord has been received by some and rejected by others, and must now make its way in an environment of suspicion and rejection. Jesus crucified is already in the glory of his father and is the Lord of Time ("Every power in heaven and on earth has been given to me," Mt

28:18), but the proof of his Resurrection remains veiled and the glory of his triumph is visible only to the eyes of faith, which are able to see beyond the shock of Good Friday and the confusion of Holy Saturday and so accept the mysterious plan of salvation which begins with the Cross ("Was it not necessary that the Messiah should suffer these things and then enter into his glory?" Lk 24:26). Our time, therefore, is the time of faith and hope; during this time we must learn to open our minds to accept the "Good News" ("Then he opened their minds to understand the Scriptures," Lk 23:43) and to broaden our horizons so that we can hope "against all hope" (Rom 4:18) when we see before us the reign of death over the human condition. In fact, "the last enemy to be destroyed is death" (1 Cor 15:26).

Our age is one which by definition exists caught between the "already" and the "not yet": Jesus has *already* risen and lives in glory, his grace has *already* begun to transform hearts and cultures, but the final, definitive victory has *not yet* come; for that we must await the Lord's return. Thus, the feelings of confusion and fear that the first disciples experienced must be opposed and overcome by the faith and hope of Mary. We need to realize just how deeply our own age is marked by suspicion and mistrust, so that the grace of Easter joy can be allowed to work on it.

## 3. The way we should live this "Sabbath of History"

It seems to me that in the anxieties and preoccupations of the disciples I recognize the anxieties and preoccupations of many believers today; this is true particularly of believers in the West, who are frequently confronted by the so-called signs of "God's defeat." In this sense, the time in which we live could be seen as a "Holy Saturday of History." How, then, should we live this special Sabbath? What is it in modern life that so confuses us? Modern life suffers from an inability to remember, the present has become fragmented, and there is a lack of vision for the future.

*a.* In the first place, we have forgotten how to *remember the past.* In actual fact, there is no lack of things that remind us of the past and that can sustain us and help us to continue on our way: both within Europe as a whole and in our own countries there are numerous symbols of considerable prestige and places of great evocative power that are associated with the long history that Christianity has in our lands—we need think no further than the great cathedrals, and places like Rome, Assisi, and so on. The Judeo-Christian tradition has also left its traces on the way we think about life, in the way we honor the dignity of the human person and seek to promote true freedom. The presence of Christianity has left indelible marks on our history.

But this type of remembrance now has a very slight hold on the way we live our daily lives. Many can find no place for this remembrance in their daily experience, and are unable to derive from it neither a sure understanding of the present nor any faith in the future. The slow yet steady progress of secularism (which manifests itself in different ways depending on a person's environment) prompts us to ask ourselves: where are we headed? In a social and cultural context in which Christianity is no longer protected and guaranteed but rather called into question, it is becoming increasingly difficult for us to live our faith: in more than a few of our social interactions it is much easier to declare yourself a nonbeliever than a believer. It does seem that nonbelief is taken for granted, while belief needs to be justified and needs to be given a legitimacy on a social level, as such legitimacy is neither obvious nor can it be taken for granted.

*b.* If our ability to remember the past diminishes, our *experience of the present* becomes disjointed and a sense of being alone takes over. Everyone feels a little lonelier.

Such loneliness is encountered above all at the level of the *family:* the relations between the couple and the relations between parents and children can be easily thrown into crisis, and everyone begins to think that perhaps they ought to learn to handle things on their own.

The ability of the great *social agencies* to bring people together and keep them together is becoming dimin-

ished, and this applies even to par-
ishes, regarding young people in particular. A fair number of movements
appear to be aging or are at least failing to replenish their ranks with new
members drawn from the rising gen-
eration.

*Political groupings* are breaking
apart, and attempts to form coalitions
suffer on account of the rebirth of fac-
tionalism. Even in those cases where
various types of voluntary activities
are carried out with great success and
dedication, one detects a certain inability to work together so as to be
more effective, to "link up" with each
other.

As a result, individuals and groups
have *no point of reference beyond themselves* and become inward looking. In
this context, it should not surprise us
to see a growing general indifference
to ethical issues and a distressing pre-
occupation with personal interests
and advantages.

We are at present witnessing a great trend towards *globalization*. It might appear that this trend corresponds to the desire that the human race grow in unity and brotherhood, witnessed to in biblical revelation. And yet this very process of the universalization of exchange—of goods, values, and persons—actually takes place within the context of a Neoliberalism and a Neocapitalism which punishes and marginalizes the weakest members of society and causes the numbers of the poor and starving to increase.

*c.* The trouble we experience in living our lives and in understanding the present colors our perception of the *future*, which appears rather bleak and uncertain as a result. We become fearful rather than expectant about the future. An indication of this is the dramatic fall in the birth rate and the decline in vocations to the priesthood and religious life. If we seek a metaphor for this fear of the future it can probably be found in the growing tendency among the young to live and to enjoy themselves at night. In such nocturnal festivities the reveler seeks to hold on to the fleeting moment, forgetting the uncertainties and the feelings of being lost that belong to the day, and avoiding confronting the demands that the today and the tomorrow bring (perhaps, and this is an avenue little explored, such activities should prompt us to reexamine the Christian tradition of the Easter Vigil and other great vigils and times of adoration, and to see that this tradition can provide real answers to the restlessness that is being expressed through this behavior).

Even that great vision of the future which is expressed in the concept of the world as a "global village" envisages for the world's tomorrow rather a unity brought about by the dominion of the strongest and most wealthy, the unity of the Tower of Babel (see Gen 11:1–9), rather than a unity of shared goods, the unity of Pentecost and of the early community in Jerusalem (see Acts 2–4).

On Good Friday, after Jesus had died, the disciple John took Mary (see Jn 19:27) into his heart and into his *home*. It is not easy to imagine just what this might mean: a house in Jerusalem? Or a simple resting place such as used by the pilgrims who came from Galilee to Jerusalem for the Passover?

I am now going to enter this house where the Mother of Jesus is spending her Holy Saturday, and with John's permission try to talk to her. The conversation is inspired first of all by contemplating the way in which Mary lived this dramatic moment.

I look at Mary: she remained in silence at the foot of the Cross in the sorrow of her Son's death; and while the body of the Crucified One lay in the tomb, she remained in silence and waiting. During this moment of her life, which was caught between the thickest darkness ("darkness came over the whole land," Mk 15:33) and the dawn of Easter Sunday ("very early on the first day after the Sabbath, when the sun had risen," Mk 16:2). Mary relived all the important "coordinates" of her life, coordinates that had shone out since the Annunciation and had marked her pilgrimage of faith. This is the way in which she speaks to our hearts, to us, pilgrims journeying through the Holy Saturday of history.

1. **Throughout the Sabbath of God's Silence you remained the *Virgo Fidelis*, and through you our minds are consoled**

What do you have to say to us, O Mother of the Lord, from the abyss of your suffering? What did you say to the confused disciples?

I seem to hear you whisper words very much like those your Son himself said one day: "If you have faith the size of a mustard seed…!" (Mt 17:20).

What do you have to tell us? It is your wish that we who have participated in your sorrow should also participate in your consolation. You know, in fact, that God "consoles us in all our affliction, so that we may be able to console those who are in any affliction with the consolation with which we ourselves are consoled by God" (2 Cor 1:4).

Such consolation comes from faith. Mary, on Holy Saturday, you are and you remain the *Virgo Fidelis*, the believing Virgin; in you the spirituality of Israel, nourished through listening and through trust, reaches its fulfillment.

But how does this consolation that

comes from the faith actually work? It comes in many different forms, and one in particular—which is greatly needed today—could be called the "consolation of the mind." What is this consolation all about?

The consolation of the mind is a very simple divine gift which allows us to grasp intuitively the richness, consistency, harmony, cohesion, and beauty of the contents of the faith at a single glance. A contemporary theologian, Hans Urs von Balthasar, calls this the "perception of the form" ("Schau der Gestalt")—an intuitive grasp of the common thread that unites all the truths of salvation and uncovers them in all their beauty and balance. We are continually faced with new examples of suffering and death which tend to weigh down on our hearts; when we find ourselves in this predicament such an intuitive grasp reveals to us the "glory of God" shining so brightly that it is able to illuminate even the darkest corners of history with the light of the truth. The consolation of the mind is the grace to perceive the Glory of God manifesting itself in the whole array of actions through which the Father gives himself to the world in the history of salvation and, in particular, in the life, death, and Resurrection of Jesus; it is the ability to see traces of the mystery of the Trinity behind and underneath all the events of our faith.

We see the gift of the consolation of the mind (or "intellectual consolation") at work when the words and actions reported in the Scriptures link up with other words and deeds from the wider Revelation: anyone who receives such a grace feels that every piece in the mosaic illuminates those near by, and that it and the pieces near and far together produce a coherent and radiant image which is thoroughly convincing. Such a person finds that one or another of the individual events in the history of salvation no longer seems to block their prayer, that they are no longer unable to see how this event or passage relates to the others and is connected to them; it seems to the person that their mind has been flooded with light, their heart expands and prayer pours forth as if from a fresh spring.

This grace, O Mary, allows those who receive it to understand God's plan mystically, to perceive it in a single glance. This plan was communicated to you by the words of the angel Gabriel when he told you about the destiny of the Son of David ("He will be great and called Son of the Most High...his reign will have no end," Lk 1:32–33). This grace allows those who receive it to contemplate, again in a single glance, the unchanging ways in which God acts, and of which you sang in the *Magnificat* (Lk 1:40–55); it is the constant meditative calling to mind of the events of our salvation which you, O Mary, practiced from the very beginning: "But Mary treasured all these words and pondered them in her heart" (Lk 2:19); "His mother treasured all these things in her heart" (Lk 2:51).

When we receive this grace, even if we receive only the merest hint of it, we experience something similar to that which the three disciples experienced on the mount of the Transfiguration. Contemplating Jesus with Moses and Elijah and hearing them speak of Jesus' "exodus" to Jerusalem (see Lk 9:21), the disciples intuitively grasped the profound ways in which the thousand episodes narrated in the Scriptures are interconnected, and they understood the strength that binds them together and brings them to fulfillment in the Passion and Resurrection of the Lord. This grace opens the eyes of our hearts and gives a profound sense of fulfillment and peace. At this moment even the shadows and tragedies of this world show themselves to be crossed by the light of love, of compassion, and of forgiveness that comes from the Father's heart. We begin to understand something of the truth of the Beatitudes, our hearts open to the hope that justice will be done, to the vision of the victory of the poor and oppressed in the world.

A saint who enjoyed this grace in an extraordinary manner, described it thus: "His intellect remained so intensely illuminated in this way that it seemed to him he was a different man, or that his intellect was different from that which it had been before. When he considered all the things he had learnt and all the graces he had received from God, and put them all together, it did not seem to him that he had learnt as much during his whole lifetime, sixty-two years of it, as he had in that single occasion" (Ignatius of Loyola, *Autobiography*, no. 30).

We do not know, O Mary, which type of profound consolation it was that sustained you during your Holy Saturday. We can be sure, however, that he who lavished such gifts on you in the decisive moments of your existence, would have, not failing in his gifts of grace, sustained you on that day, too. It was the strength of the Spirit, present in you since the very beginning, which supported you in the moment of darkness and of Jesus' apparent defeat. You received the gift to believe completely in God's plan, and you saw its power and glory in your innermost depths. Thus, you teach us how to believe even when we are passing through the nights of our faith, how to sing the praises of the Most High's glory while we are experiencing abandonment, and to proclaim the primacy of God and to love him in his silences and when he appears to be defeated. Intercede for us, O Mother, so that we may not lack that consolation of our minds which sustains our faith, so that the birds of the air can come and make nests in the branches of the tree that has grown from a grain of mustard seed (see Mt 13:31–32).

## 2. Throughout the Sabbath of Disappointment you were the Mother of Hope, and through you our hearts are consoled

What more do you have to say to us, O Mary, from the silence that envelops you? I hear you repeat, as if a sigh, the words of your Son: "By your perseverance you will gain your souls" (Lk 21:19).

The word "perseverance" can also be translated as "patience." Patience and perseverance are the virtues of the one who waits, who does not yet see, but continues to hope: these virtues sustain us when we are faced with "the scoffers who say: 'Where is the promise of his coming? For ever since our ancestors died, all things continue as they were from the beginning of creation!'" (2 Pet 3:3–4).

You learnt, O Mary, to wait and to hope. You waited with trust for the birth of the Son that the angel proclaimed; you continued to believe in the word of Gabriel, even during those long periods of time when you understood nothing; you hoped against every hope under the Cross and right up to the Sepulchre itself; during Holy Saturday you instilled hope into the confused and disappointed disciples. Through you, the disciples were given the consolation of hope, the consolation that could be called the "consolation of the heart," and through you our hearts are consoled too.

If the consolation of the mind illuminates our intellect and "opens our eyes" (see Lk 24:31), the consolation of the heart (see Lk 24:32)—or "affective consolation"—touches us on the level of our sensitivity and our profound affections, disposing them to adhere to God's promises, overcoming impatience and disappointment. When the Lord seems slow in fulfilling his promises, this grace enables us to withstand in hope and to persevere in our waiting. Such consolation is the "living hope" of which Peter speaks (see 1 Pet 1:3), and the "hope against every hope" of which Paul speaks in connection with Abraham: "No distrust made him waver concerning the promise of God, but he grew strong in his faith as he gave glory to God, being fully convinced that God was able to do what he had promised" (Rom 4:20–21).

You waited patiently and in peace, O Mother of God, on Holy Saturday; you teach us to watch in patience and perseverance how we are living this

Sabbath of History when many—Christians among them—are tempted to abandon their hope in eternal life and in the Lord's return. The impatience and haste which characterize our technological culture make it difficult for us to accept that we might have to wait until God's plan is fully revealed and the Risen One is finally victorious. The little faith we have and the fact that we lack the ability to read the signs of God's presence in history prompt in us an impatience and a desire to run away; this is exactly what happened in the case of the two who journeyed to Emmaus—who, even though they were given certain signs of the Risen One, did not have the strength to accept the way events were unfolding and so left Jerusalem (see Lk 24:13ff).

We turn to you, O Mother of hope and of patience: ask your Son that he might have mercy on us, and come and search for us down the roads we take in our impatience and our desire to run away, as he did for the disciples of Emmaus. Ask him to make our hearts burn within us once more (see Lk 24:32).

Intercede for us so that we will be able to live in time, yet filled with the hope of eternity, with the certainty that God's plan for the world will reach fulfillment in its own time, so that we will be able to contemplate with joy the glory of the Risen One, glory that is already present in the mystery of history, though hidden behind a veil.

3. Throughout the Sabbath of Absence and of Solitude you remained the Mother of Love, and through you our lives are consoled

At this point, O Mary, I would like to hazard a final question: what meaning does all your suffering have? How could you remain firm while your Son's friends fled, were scattered, and went into hiding? How were you able to give meaning to the tragedy that you experienced? It seems to me that again you respond with the words of your Son: "unless a grain of wheat falls into the earth and dies, it remains just a single grain; but if it dies, it bears much fruit" (Jn 12:24).

Your suffering found its meaning, O Mary, in the creation of a people of believers. On Holy Saturday you were revealed as the loving Mother who brings forth her children under the shadow of the Cross, understanding intuitively that neither your sacrifice nor that of your Son are in vain. If he loved us and gave himself for us (see Gal 2:20), if the Father did not spare him but gave him up for all of us (see Rom 8:32), you united your mother's heart to the boundless charity of God, certain of its fruitfulness. From this a people was born, "a great multitude…from every nation, from all tribes and peoples and languages" (Rev 7:9); the Beloved Disciple, who was entrusted to you at the foot of the Cross ("Woman, behold your Son," Jn 19:26) symbolizes this multitude.

The consolation with which God sustained you on Holy Saturday, with Jesus absent and the disciples scattered, is an inner strength of which we are not necessarily conscious, but whose presence and effect is known by its fruits, by its spiritual fruitfulness. And we, here and now, O Mary, are the children born from your suffering.

We have all had the experience of being able to perceive the presence of a strength that accompanied us in times of difficulty, even if we did not feel it when we suffered and it seemed to us that we did not possess it. It may seem to us sometimes that we have been abandoned by God and by our fellow human beings, and yet, when we look back over the events that have just passed we realize that the Lord had continued to walk with us, and had even carried us in his arms. This experience might remind us of what happened to Moses on Mount Horeb: he was allowed to see something of the glory of God which he had so desired to behold ("Show me your glory!" Ex 33:18), but only when it had already passed him by (see Ex 33:19–22).

Such consolation is at work in us and sustains us very effectively, even though we may have no awareness of our minds being illuminated and no sense of being moved in the depths of our heart; it is at work in us, giving us the strength to hold on in times of trial, when all around us is dark. I call it a "substantial consolation" because it touches the depth and the very substance of our soul, well beneath our conscious and more superficial impulses; alternatively, it could be called a "consolation of life," because it makes its effects felt in our everyday lives, helping us to stand firm during the most difficult moments ("so that you may be able to withstand on that evil day," Eph 6:13), when our minds seem shrouded in darkness.

You know, O Mary, probably through personal experience, that the darkness of Holy Saturday can sometimes penetrate right into the depths of our soul, even though our will may be completely devoted to God's plan. You obtain for us this consolation which sustains our spirits without our realizing it; you will allow us, at the right time, to see the fruits of our "holding fast," and you pray that we may become spiritually fruitful. One can never repent of having persevered in love! We will realize, then, that we have had an experience similar to that described by Paul when he wrote to the Corinthians: "So death is at work in us, but life in you" (2 Cor 4:12).

You, O Mary, are the Mother of Sorrows, you are the one who did not cease to love God, even though he appeared to be absent, and in God you never tire of loving his children, watching over them in the silence of waiting. During your Holy Saturday, O Mary, you became the icon of the Church of Love, sustained by a faith stronger than death and living in the charity which overcomes abandonment. Obtain for us, O Mary, that profound consolation that enables us to love even in the night of faith and of hope, when in the darkness it seems to us that we cannot even see the face of our neighbor!

You teach us, O Mary, that there is a "high price" to pay for the apostolate, the proclamation of the Gospel, pastoral work, the task of educating others in the faith to create a people of believers. Thus Jesus acquired us: "You know that you were ransomed from the futile ways inherited from your ancestors, not with perishable things like silver or gold, but with the precious blood of Christ" (1 Pet 1:18–19). Grant us that innermost consolation of life that allows us to pay this price of salvation willingly, in union with the heart of Christ.

# III

Moving
Towards
the Eighth
Day
During
the Sabbath
of Time

I n the first part of this letter, I pro-
posed that we should try to recognize in ourselves the same confusion
that the disciples experienced on the
day following Jesus' death. In the second, I attempted to contemplate with
you the faith, hope, and charity of the
Madonna of Holy Saturday. In this final part, I would like to bring these
two moments within the history of
salvation together to see how they
interact, and then try to understand
how the light of the witness given by
Mary and the consolations that we receive from her Son through her might
illuminate our own uncertainties and
guide our path.

If our encounter with the fright-
ened disciples has helped us to recognize the reality of our own fears, of

the resistance to God that we experience both around us and in our own selves, and of our sin, then the faith, hope and charity of Mary can help us to understand that time—even the time in which we live—is in fact like one great "Sabbath." And in this Sabbath we live caught between the "already" of the Lord's first coming and the "not yet" of his return, like pilgrims journeying towards the "eighth day," the Sunday on which the sun does not set, which he himself will come to open at the end of time.

## 1. Looking at the past with the eyes of faith

The disciples of Holy Saturday bore within them the memory of all they had experienced with their Master. Yet these recollections were filled with nostalgia and were a source of sadness; all the hopes they had shared with him and all the expectations they had placed in him seemed to be irretrievably lost.

We too carry the memory of our Christian past very deeply inside ourselves: we need look no further than our own culture, marked by the great values of biblical tradition—from the idea of the "person" to the notion of "time" understood as history moving towards a fulfillment, both promised and expected. Our important spaces are filled with traces of this memory: from works of art, often with religious subject matter, to our churches and the Duomo [in Milan] which is a symbol of not only the local Church but of a far wider secular identification with the figure of Saint Ambrose.

As in the case of the disciples on the road to Emmaus, still totally lost in their Holy Saturday, the memory of such roots could be for us a cause of nothing but nostalgia and sadness: this sort of memory is inactive and incapable of filling us with energy and inspiring us to fresh undertakings in which we discover generosity and passion. For the Madonna of Holy Saturday, however, these very memories became a source of prophecy: she remembered in order to hope, she revisited the past in order to open herself to the future. This she did in the certainty that God is faithful to his promises and that all that he did in her through the birth of her eternal Son in time, he will do likewise to bring Jesus and his brothers and sisters to rebirth from death to the life on which the sun does not set.

Mary "treasured all these things in her heart" (Lk 2:51). She merits well the praise given in the Gospel, "Woman, great is your faith! Let it be done for you as you wish" (Mt 15:28), and she understands how to marry the past of the Lord's wonders with the future that the Lord alone causes to come about. Her hymn of praise, the *Magnificat*, expresses in the past tense ("He has shown strength with his arm," Lk 1:5 1ff) the certainty she feels about the future. The Madonna of Holy Saturday teaches us how to recover the sense that memory is not only an element of tradition, but also and especially something which spurs us on to move forward. At the school of her faith, rich in hope, we must ask ourselves how we can give value to the great traditions of the past that the Church possesses, and make them relevant to the present day.

In this context I think of our Church's artistic heritage, and I ask myself how these treasures could become a way of announcing the Gospel in a world that feels the need for beauty so deeply.

I think also—to name but one more significant example of the same—of the extremely rich tradition of the Oratories [a recreation area for the young people of the parish where religious instruction is often given], a part of the Italian people's journey in faith of which we are justifiably proud. I ask myself how the Oratories could respond evermore better to the restlessness and challenges of the younger generations, who continually seek a way out from the monotony of their daily duties in their nightly festivities which are filled with the loud sounds of the rock music and with actions and gestures that often seem vain and incomprehensible to adults.

I think especially of the Sacred Scriptures, that privileged place where the memory of the *mirabilia Dei*, the miraculous works of God, is recorded. The grace of the consolation of the mind, which helps us to understand the full meaning of the events of this world, is very closely connected with the prayerful reading of the Bible, the *lectio divina*. Whoever is faithful to a faith-inspired reading of the Scriptures receives from the Spirit the gift of being able to proceed with joy and trust through the difficult and inexplicable moments of history, and can see God's plan for the salvation of humankind clearly in them all.

## 2. The hope which opens up the future

The disciples spent Holy Saturday in fear, and in the dread that something worse was coming; the future seemed to have nothing but defeat and growing humiliation in store for them. Mary, on the other hand, waited in trust and patience; she knew that God's promises would be fulfilled.

In the Sabbath of Time in which we find ourselves we, too, must learn to rediscover the importance of waiting; the absence of hope, perhaps, represents the terminal illness of the conscience in an age which is marked by the end of all ideological dreams and the aspirations connected with them.

Hope alone is the antidote to indifference and frustration, to the habit of living exclusively for the present moment, without any expectation for the future. It is not the kind of hope that is based on calculations, forecasts, and statistics, but the sort which is founded solely on God's promises. Once again the Madonna of Holy Saturday casts light on the task that awaits us, a task which lies within our power because the Risen One has given us his Spirit, which touches us inside through the consolation of the heart. Through simple actions in our daily lives we can, without forcing anything, light up the world around us with the inner joy and peace which are the fruits of the consolation of the Spirit.

Believing in Christ, who died and rose for us, means becoming witnesses to hope through our words and our lives.

Through our words: we must not

be afraid to approach the great themes which are relevant to our final hope: eternal life and the Last Things that are part of it (death, judgment, heaven, purgatory and hell; in connection with this subject see my Pastoral Letter [of 1992–94], *I Stand at the Door*).

Through our lives we are called to give clear and credible witness to the light that ultimate values cast on penultimate values, making life choices inspired by the humility and patience of Christ, choices which are characterized by sobriety, poverty, and chastity. Through such choices, shared ever more widely, the general tendency to globalization that we have talked about will receive the correction it needs to prevent it from becoming a deadly root of exclusion and marginalization of the increasingly poor; this tendency will instead help to promote an ever-growing inclusion of all in the exchange of produced goods, in a spirit of mutual agreement. Here, too, the "strong woman" (see Prov 31:10) of Holy Saturday is a model and source of help—she has shown us how to hope against all hope and to believe in the impossible possibility of God beyond all the evidence of his defeat.

## 3. The charity which gives us back the present

During Holy Saturday the disciples experienced the present as heavy with tension, and their overwhelming experience was a sense of the solitude in which the death of Jesus had left them—he who had been the basis of their communion.

It does not take much to realize that this experience of solitude is rife among Christians today. It is most noticeable on a *personal* level, where hearts are lacerated when faced with no future, no meaning and their inability to enter into dialogue with the other. We can also see it in the many ways in which *family life* is breaking up; in the difficulty parish *communities* and movements and associations are experiencing in their recruitment of new members and retention of existing ones; in the disjointed nature of *political life* itself, evidenced by the difference between "representation" and actual "representing" (the elected representatives of the people often do not represent the real needs and interests of those who have elected them) and—in the Catholic world— by the diaspora that followed the end of Catholic political unity.

Mary was able to retain not only the memory of *communion* but also the charity to live it in the present. She stayed with the disciples, she comforted them, reunited them, encouraged them, enabling them to taste the fruits of that consolation of life which creates communion; during God's silence and the apparent defeat of Love Crucified she held them together; she was a witness to compassionate love and to an active solidarity; in the Upper Room she prepared herself, already full of the Holy Spirit, to receive with the disciples the gift of the new beginning made possible by the death of Jesus. At Mary's school we cannot avoid asking ourselves how we should live our present condition in the light that the Risen One throws on the Sabbath of Time through which we are living. In fact, during the "Church's journey/pilgrimage through space and time, and even more through the story of our souls, Mary is present" (John Paul II, *Redemptoris Mater*, no. 25).

On the level of our *personal existence*, the school of Mary can help us to overcome the temptation to anxiety and to live our lives with trust and eagerness before the Eternal One—to rediscover life itself as a vocation, which is to be lived with the faith in God and faithfulness that God's own faithfulness makes possible. This is the only way in which the discernment of vocations, so necessary for individuals and for the community's urgent needs, finds an adequate setting. Through prayer we can catch hold, with the Madonna, of the grace of the consolation of life that makes it possible to persevere and to remain faithful until death to the word we gave when we dedicated ourselves to God.

Regarding *communion within the family*, it seems to me that the light of Mary's charity asks us to rediscover charity between spouses and within the family, and to proclaim it ever more insistently both in and out of season; such charity is capable of inspiring our response to the vocation of marriage and the faithfulness, new every morning, to the covenant confirmed in the sacrament of marriage. Without a "gratuitous" love, nourished by the springs of grace, it is not possible to live the ongoing and reciprocal self-giving that life as a couple requires; nor is it possible to spend yourself in the personal sacrifice required to ensure that family life is experienced as a place of freedom, growth, and truth. The challenge that is presented by the current crisis in conjugal and parental relations can be faced and overcome through repeated reciprocal forgiveness and charity.

Similarly, the *communion in the life of the Church*—at all levels, from the parish to the diocese, from movements to associations—requires us to make that leap of charity that the Madonna of Holy Saturday made: we must all welcome and forgive each other following the Lord's example. In his request for forgiveness in the name of the whole Church and in his personal offer of forgiveness to his assailant, the Pope has given us a remarkable witness of this.

We must learn to enter into dialogue with each other and with all people. I think of the constant need for creative energy and new ideas in the life of communal parish and diocesan organizations—and here the presence of lay pastoral workers, increasingly better led, supported, and trained, will be decisive. I think—following the mind of the Universal Church of which it is impossible not to feel a living member—of the urgency to jointly confront and resolve on a truly Catholic level the great challenges presented by life today; this applies on both a world level and on a level that concerns specifically our own society in Europe (this was the sense of the third "dream" of which I spoke at the European Synod of October 1999). I think of the promotion *of ecumenical dialogue*—the recent declaration of Augsburg by Catholics and Lutherans on justification is a precious fruit of this. I think of *interreli-*

*gious dialogue*, which appears to have an unavoidable urgency, not only because of the growing presence among us of immigrants belonging to different religious worlds from ourselves, but also because of the responsibility believers of all faiths in God have to give witness together to God's primacy over life and history and thus contribute to the foundation of a shared behavior, with an ethical responsibility towards others.

Such dialogue and the charity that should inspire it are urgently needed in the relations between *civil society* and *political representatives:* we were reminded of this need recently in the last Italian Catholic Social Week, celebrated at Naples during November 1999, which focused its attention on the relations necessary—with all the proper distinctions—between political mediation, institutions, and civil society in the country. If in the past a passive logic of delegation prevailed, today we often see a disturbing detachment between political and ecclesiastical life, ethics, and public service, and personal and collective interests. In the "Sabbath of Politics," too, it is necessary to allow a few rays from the Sunday of Resurrection to shine forth. We must learn to educate ourselves both to the exercise of political charity and to the promotion of the dialogue which takes place between groups (which are the very fabric of civil society and often the ways in which the Church community expresses itself) and those who are active in political mediation or are called to work for the common good in institutions.

Finally, we must learn to discover and follow paths of reconciliation in all that concerns the relations between *humankind and creation:* the wounds that exist within ourselves and our relations with others are reflected in the lack of balance between ourselves and nature, as history so often records. The ecological crisis consists precisely in the imbalance caused by the contrast between biological rhythms and those imposed by humankind: these—through the technological and scientific means which we have at our disposal today—can modify in a rapid and irreversible manner what nature has taken millennia and often millions of years to produce. The moderate use by each one of us of all that technology puts at our disposal is clearly an increasingly urgent and necessary task as the process of globalization gains momentum: here also the awareness that we are living through time's Sabbath and not the day of its fulfillment ought to induce us to make balanced choices, choices which show we are capable of exercising self-restraint in matters of knowledge and power so as to increase the quality of life of all and for all.

For these new paths on which we

must embark, I rely on the capacity of our young people to generate new ideas and to lead the way; our young people know how to look to Mary's example, and I would like her example to be a call to assume their responsibility for the future in this respect.

## 4. Where are we? Where are we heading?

We find ourselves, then, in the Sabbath of Time, on our way to the eighth day: between the "already" and the "not yet" we must avoid seeing the present day as the be-all and end-all, in an attitude of either triumphalism, or of defeatism. We cannot allow ourselves to grind to a halt in the darkness of Good Friday, in a sort of "Christianity without redemption"; nor can we seek to hasten in ourselves the full revelation of the Easter victory that will be fulfilled in the Second Coming of the Son of Man.

We are invited to live as pilgrims in the night which has been illuminated by the hope of faith and warmed by the authenticity of love. The Jubilee Year, in this sense, is a new dawn that lies between the renewed remembrance of God's wonders and the expectation of their final fulfillment; it nourishes our commitment, renews our energies, and makes us feel that, together with Christ (see Col 3:3), we are indeed kept in the bosom of the Father with Mary, like Mary, on the Holy Saturday of her faith which was so rich in charity.

Then it will seem to us that the Sabbath of Time is already colored by the light of the promised dawn, and the pale light of our passing days will be made more radiant through the first rays of the day that has no end; this day is the eighth and last day, the first day of the eternal life of all those who have risen in the Risen One.

Each year the celebration of the

Paschal Triduum accompanies us and enlightens us along this journey of re-membrance. Through the richness of its words and actions, the Triduum encourages the Church every time to see herself within the entire plan of salvation, to understand which direction she should take and what kind of future she should prepare for. I invite you to celebrate the Paschal Triduum in this sort of spiritual atmosphere; prepare yourself carefully, remaining true to our attempts of the last few years to re-propose it, which was done in an attempt to regain the attention of our communities.

Our celebration, rooted in our rich Ambrosian liturgical tradition, becomes like an entrance into the Sabbath of Time, which Sabbath is summed up in the Passover of Jesus; and so we are able to draw on its rich meaning and live by the grace that it liberates. Let us set out with ever greater conviction to celebrate and experience all the liturgical seasons with this awareness, beginning with the Sunday liturgy. Thus we will find in our celebrations help to overcome the confusion that assails us and to experience the luminous grace that illumined Mary's Holy Saturday.

## 5. An attempt at a balance sheet: an appointment and an invitation

Looking back over the three weeks of years, to use a scriptural image (see Lev 25:8) during which I have served here in Milan, I would that all that really was the center and the heart of all our words and pastoral undertakings might become clear; I would that all that the Spirit has said to our Church during my time of service might become simple and clear to all.

To achieve this, I need the help of you all, and so I close this letter—which is "Sabbatical" in more sense than one—by extending an invitation to you. I would ask you, both as individuals and as a community, to answer the following question: what in particular has helped us during all these years to walk and to grow in the Father's love, in the grace of Christ and the communion of the Holy Spirit? What from our two decades along the road together, remains living and life-giving? What has the Spirit said to our Church here in Milan?

It would be nice if the responses were to be the fruit of prayer: then you could write down what the Lord suggested to you and give it to me. Using these contributions I will then attempt to produce something like a "balance sheet" in the form of a *Confessio laudis, vitae et fidei*.

May the Madonna whose generous faith during Holy Saturday has been at the heart of this letter and whose witness and intercession has accompanied my pastoral service, help us in this "self-examination." I entrust myself to her once again, along with you, in the Jubilee Year of her Son s incarnation, who is our Savior and the Redeemer of humankind.

Carlo-Maria Martini,
Archbishop of Milan
Feast of the Transfiguration of the Lord
*August 6, 2000,*
*On the 22nd anniversary of the death of Paul VI*